body decoration

Adam Sutherland

Lerner Publications Company
Minneapolis

First American edition published in 2012 by Lerner Publishing Group, Inc. Published by arrangement with Wayland, a division of Hachette Children's Books

Lerner Publications Company
A division of Lerner Publishing Group, Inc.
241 First Avenue North
Minneapolis, MN U.S.A.

Website address: www.lernerbooks.com

Library of Congress Cataloging-in-Publication Data

Sutherland, Adam.
    Body decoration / by Adam Sutherland.
      p.   cm. — (On the radar : street style)
    Includes index.
    ISBN 978-0-7613-7769-6 (lib. bdg. : alk. paper)
    1. Body marking—Juvenile literature. I. Title.
GN419.15.S88 2012
391.6'5—dc23   2011023396

Manufactured in the United States of America
 – CG – 12/31/11

Acknowledgments: Corbis: Reuters 24l; iStockphoto: Luca Cepparo cover; RexFeatures: F1 Online 25l, Sipa Press 28; Shutterstock: 1171 6bl, Kharidehal Abhirama Ashwin 9br, AISPIX 18tr, Andrey Arkusha 8br, Lucian Coman 18cl, Kobby Dagan 11, Lev Dolgachov 19tl, Olga Ekaterincheva 23cr, Helga Esteb 2b, 26, Icons Jewelry 2–3, Iofoto 13br, Elena Itsenko 15br, Nicky Jacobs 22tr, Donald Joski 23t, Andy Lim 30–31, Vasilchenko Nikita 15bc, Ostill 3tr, Dmitriy Pochitalin 1, PZAxe 15bl, Omer N Raja 24r, Pavel Reband 25r, Rsfatt 12cl, Alexey Stiop 4–5, StockHouse 12br, Mikhail Tchkheidze 23bl, Timur G 3br, Dusaleev Viatcheslav 7tr, VSO 29tr, Vladimir Wrangel 0; Wikimedia: Kahuroa 2c, 8l; Orla Zusman: 3tl, 15t.

Main body text set in
Helvetica Neue LT Std 13/15.5.

cover stories

14
FIVE-MINUTE INTERVIEW
Find out from On the Radar's expert Orla Zusman why nail art is so popular.

8, 10
THE BACK STORY
Take a look at the fascinating history of body decoration.

16, 20
SHOW ME
Create beautiful nail flowers and make your own earrings with our photo guides!

26
STAR STORY
Chart the rise of TV tattoo artist Kat Von D.

the people

the art

the talk

BODIES, INC.

Body decoration takes place in all cultures. From pierced ears to nail art to colorful tattoos, millions of people decorate their bodies to enhance their look.

Colorful nail art

Many people wear colorful designs on their fingernails and toenails. A worldwide industry of nail bars has appeared to fulfill this demand.

Hair flair

People from many cultures have enhanced their hair in dramatic ways. Many people lengthen their hair with extensions or weaves, grow it into thick dreadlocks, or use hair dye and styling gels.

Earrings and beyond!

Ear piercing is the most common form of body piercing, with lips, noses, and tongues following close behind. Others go beyond piercing and stretch their earlobes for a more dramatic look.

Paint power

Cosmetic makeup has always been the most widely used form of body decoration. Face and body painting used to be done with clay, charcoal, or henna. Modern-day artists create amazing, colorful designs with specially made paints.

Skin deep

The practice of tattooing grew out of traditional African and Native American markings. Tattooing has become a big business. There are even television shows dedicated to tattoo artists and their clients!

BODY TALK

Decorate your vocabulary
with our On the Radar guide!

body painting
decorating the body with
paint specially created
for use on the skin

cornrows
a West African hairstyle in
which flat braids are worn
close to the head

cosmetics
beauty products; from a
Greek word that means
"skilled in adornment"

dreadlocks
a Jamaican hairstyle in which
long hair is worn in thick,
ropelike strands

ear piercing

hair extension
artificial bits of hair that are
secured to a person's scalp to
add length, volume, or texture

harquus
a temporary ink tattoo based
on patterns commonly used
by women in North Africa, the
Middle East, and South Asia

henna
a reddish dye made from the
powdered leaves of a plant

jewelry wire
thin, bendable wire in shades
of silver, bronze, or gold that
can be used to create jewelry

kohl
a cosmetic first used by
ancient Egyptian women
to darken the edges of the
eyelids

lead paint
a type of paint that contains
the heavy metal lead to
promote drying and make
color last. It can seriously harm
skin and has been banned for
most domestic uses.

Mohawk
a hairstyle in which the sides
of the head are often shaved,
while the center is grown long
and styled into a stiff shape

nail bar
a beauty salon that
specializes in manicures
(fingernail grooming),
pedicures (toenail grooming),
and specialized nail designs

rouge
red or pink makeup put on
cheeks to make them look
less pale

skinhead
a British hairstyle in which the
hair is shaved close to the
head. Later, the term came to
mean someone wearing the
hairstyle who belonged to a
violent gang.

sleeve
a tattoo that covers a
person's arm from the wrist
to the shoulder

GLOSSARY

body painting

antisocial
behaving in a way that upsets
or harms others

arthritis
a painful condition in which
the joints of the body swell

**Black Power
movement**
efforts that started in the
1960s to improve political
and economic conditions for
African Americans

commemorate
an act carried out to remember
something or someone

condemn
to strongly disapprove
of something

convention
a large meeting of a group
with shared interests

dermis
the deep inner layer of the
skin, containing blood vessels

distinctive
something that is
eye-catching or
instantly recognizable

hip-hop
a style of dance, music, and
dress that originated in New
York City in the 1960s

insoluble
not able to be dissolved

mainstream
a part of popular culture

Mohawk
a Native American group that
lived in a river valley, later
named the Mohawk Valley, in
upstate New York

noninvasive
a procedure accomplished
without piercing the skin or
leaving permanent marks

penetrate
to pierce, enter, or push
through something

puncture
to make a hole with a sharp
object

punk
a style of music and dress that
started in the late 1970s

Rastafarian
a member of a Jamaican
religion

sterile
free from bacteria

subculture
a small part of mainstream
culture, with its own attitudes,
beliefs, and influences

superstition
a belief that a person's actions
can influence the outcome of a
future event

underground
hidden or secret; not well
known to many people

7

ANCIENT MARKINGS

The Maori people of New Zealand tattooed their bodies to show their status within a tribe. The tattoos of this sixteenth-century Maori chief display his importance.

Body decoration has been around almost as long as the human race. Historians believe that tattooing goes back at least 10,000 years. Piercing dates back 4,000 years. Tribes in Asia and Europe had their own preferred markings, depending on their superstitions or their rank in society.

Ear ornaments

The oldest earrings date back to 2500 B.C. and were found in a grave in Iraq. Metal earrings were originally thought to prevent spirits from entering the body through the ears. Later, earrings became a symbol of wealth. Ancient Romans wore precious stones in their ears, and the ancient Egyptians wore expensive gold hoops.

Oldest ink

The oldest recorded tattoos belong to Ötzi the Iceman, who died around 3300 B.C. His preserved body was found in the Austrian Alps in 1991. Some of his 57 tattoos are believed to be for tribal or religious purposes. Others are thought to have been for the treatment of arthritis! Tattooed 2,500-year-old Egyptian mummies have also been discovered.

Tahitian "tatau"

The word *tatau,* or tattoo, originated in Tahiti, an island in the South Pacific Ocean. British explorer Captain James Cook traveled to Tahiti twice between 1768 and 1775. There, he met tribesmen covered with traditional markings. Their skin was cut with sharp tools that were then dipped in ink and tapped into the skin.

Rings and things

Lip piercing was thought to have been practiced by Eskimos in the Arctic Circle around 3500 B.C. as a sign of status. Nose piercing was first recorded in Iraq and Iran 4,000 years ago. Travelers to the region from Europe and the United States brought back the practice of nose piercing in the 1960s. The Aztecs originally performed tongue piercing to draw blood for the gods.

Stained skin

Henna comes from a plant that grows naturally in the Middle East and India. It has been used as a body decoration for more than 5,000 years. The plant can be ground into a paste and left on skin to temporarily stain it with a reddish color. Henna was believed to bring luck. It is still used in many parts of the world in festivals and celebrations. Indian brides decorate their hands, palms, and fingernails with henna. (Applying black henna, however, can cause scarring.)

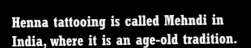

Henna tattooing is called Mehndi in India, where it is an age-old tradition.

PAINTED FACES

Makeup isn't a modern invention. In fact, cosmetics—particularly lipstick, eyeliner, and foundation—were used by the ancient Egyptians as far back as 4000 B.C. Some early cosmetics were made from crushed plants and other harmless substances. Others contained poisons that had harmful effects on the wearer!

This bust of the ancient Egyptian queen Nefertiti shows her eyes heavily lined with kohl.

Ancient eyes

Ancient Egyptians outlined their eyes with a substance called kohl. It was made from a mixture of lead, copper, burned almonds, soot, and other ingredients. The Egyptians believed that eye makeup could improve eyesight and ward off evil spirits. In ancient Rome, cosmetics were usually made by special female slaves called Cosmetae.

Early nail polish

The Chinese began to stain their fingernails with a mixture of gelatin, beeswax, and egg starting around 3000 B.C. They used different colors, depending on their social class. Zhou dynasty royals wore gold and silver. Later royals wore black or red. The lower classes were forbidden from wearing royal colors.

Geisha makeup

In Japan, traditional female entertainers called geisha color their faces and necks white using rice powder. They sometimes mix it with bird droppings for a lighter color! They then paint their eyebrows, lips, and eyelids with a paste made from crushed flower petals.

Victorian ladies

Wealthy nineteenth-century ladies also preferred pale skin. Makeup was rarely used, although cheeks were sometimes reddened with rouge, a colored powder made from beetroot. Fine blue lines were often painted on the skin to increase the appearance of delicate skin with veins showing through!

Along with their distinctive makeup, geisha also wear elaborate hair decorations, including decorative combs and fabric flowers.

Perfect pale skin

Between the fourteenth and seventeenth centuries, the European working classes often farmed the land, and so their skin became tanned from the sun. For the European upper classes, pale skin became a sign of wealth and social status. Both men and women artificially lightened their skin. White lead paint was one of the methods they used. It contained a poison called arsenic, which killed many of its users.

Modern makeup

In the early 1900s, makeup became fashionable in the United States and Europe thanks to its widespread use in the fields of ballet, theater, and film. Mass-market cosmetics companies—such as Max Factor, Elizabeth Arden, L'Oréal, and Helena Rubinstein—became household names.

COOL OR FOOL?

Body decoration divides public opinion. Supporters say that it is a positive expression of individuality. They believe:

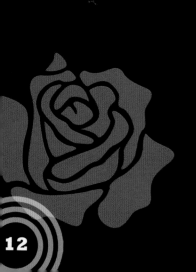

1. Body decoration involves freedom of expression. People should be free to adorn their own bodies in whatever way they want.
2. To condemn body decoration is to condemn thousands of years of tradition and beliefs in many cultures around the world.
3. Tattooing is an art form in its own right. Many tattoo artists are respected for their work, in the same way as more traditional artists. Tattoo designs have made their way into fashion and art galleries.
4. Some forms of body decoration are noninvasive and temporary and so are no different from putting on makeup.
5. Extreme hairstyles, piercings, or tattoos can indicate membership of a social group. They can help people to feel part of a subculture and give them a sense of purpose and belonging.
6. Children as young as three are often encouraged to wear face paint or have temporary tattoos. Why should it be so different for teenagers or adults?

Some people are strongly opposed to others adorning their bodies and changing their appearance. They say:

1. Piercings, tattoos, and extreme hairstyles can appear to be antisocial or even threatening.
2. Piercings can be dangerous. They can get caught, ripped out, or even become infected. Some people have died after multiple body piercings.
3. If tattoos are not expertly done using sterile needles, they can become infected. People have been known to get diseases from this art form.
4. A tattoo is meant to be permanent. If a person decides he or she no longer likes it, removing it is an expensive and painful process. Once removed, the skin is still scarred.
5. Permanent types of body decoration can seem like a good idea when you are young. Years later, they may look inappropriate or strange.

AGAINST

RIGHT OR WRONG?

Body decoration is an ancient tradition that is still respected in many cultures. However, it can look threatening and can be off-putting to certain sections of society. As a result, people with lots of tattoos and piercings can find it hard to be accepted. Body decoration is not for everyone, but in many societies, people are allowed to express themselves freely, as long as they are not harming others.

ORLA ZUSMAN

Orla works as a nail artist for Nails, Inc., a nail bar chain. Here, she tells On the Radar readers why she loves her job.

What did you learn at school?

We were taught the science of nails—how they grow and how diet can affect them. We then practiced shaping the nails and moved on to painting and decorating them. We started learning with dark colors. They are harder to apply, because the nail varnish is thicker. If you make a mistake, it's more obvious!

Why did you choose nails as a career?

I've always loved art, and I love to express myself! I also enjoy meeting new people. Every day is different. It's a challenge creating new styles and designs for each person.

Why do you think nail art is so popular now?

Firstly, nail art is relatively inexpensive. Secondly, it's not permanent—you can change your design to match your outfit! Lastly, I would say that because nail bars are so common, it is also much more accessible.

What makes a good nail artist?

You need to be creative, and you also need to have a strong opinion. Clients will often come in and not know how they want their nails to look. It's my job to talk to them, find out more about them, and suggest ideas that I think match their personality. Some people want to follow the latest trends. Others prefer more classic, timeless designs.

How long is your working day?

I usually do six- or eight-hour shifts. But I often get carried away on a client's design and end up staying longer.

Why do you think people like such eye-catching designs?

I think it's great to feel special, or unique, particularly for an important occasion. One of my customers came in for a design for her daughter's wedding day. She chose a circle of crystals on her own ring finger to commemorate the day.

What are the most common nail designs?

Crystals are very popular. We add tiny gems to the nails to create amazing designs. We also get asked to create initials, half-moon shapes, and glitter work. Recently, a lot of people have been asking for animal print designs. We use different colors to apply zebra or leopard prints to the nails.

NAIL FLOWERS

Nail art is a fun and easy way to turn your hands into temporary works of art!

You will need:

- base coat varnish
- 2 colors of nail varnish
- bobby pin
- clear nail varnish

1 On clean, dry hands, paint a clear base coat. Let this dry completely.

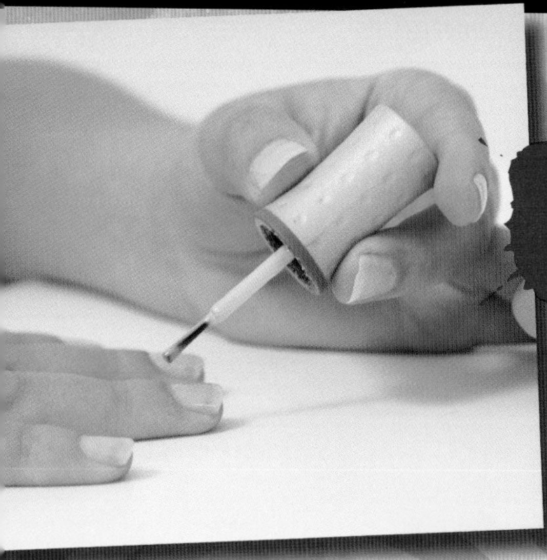

2 Paint your chosen background color. Let this dry completely. If it is still wet when you follow with the later steps, it will smear.

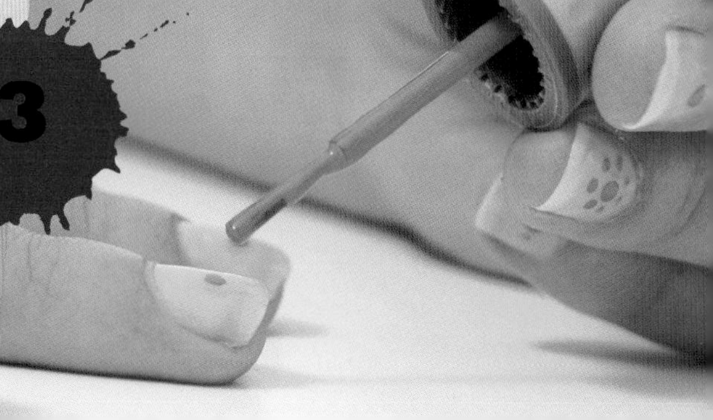

3 Make a dot in the middle of each nail with your second varnish color.

4

Unbend the bobby pin. Use one end to put five small dots of varnish around the dot in the center of each nail. This will make a flower pattern. Let the varnish dry completely.

5

When the flower is completely dry, paint your nails with clear nail varnish.

Got it?

Once you have mastered the basic nail flower, be adventurous and try different colored flowers on each nail, or even flowers with five different colored petals!

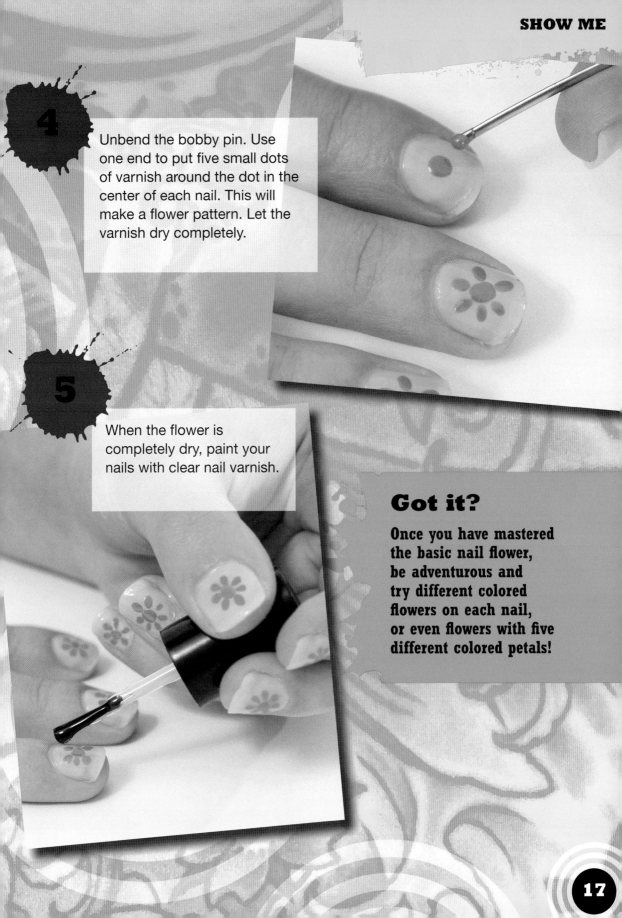

HAIR-RAISING STYLES

skinhead

cornrows

Mohawk

dreadlocks

Body decoration goes beyond the skin. A distinctive hairstyle is one obvious way to show imagination, originality, creativity, and self-expression. Here are some of the most well-known and popular styles.

Simply shaved

The skinhead hairstyle, with hair cut extremely short or even shaved off completely, started in Britain in the 1960s. The style soon spread to other parts of the world. Both men and women wore the style. Although the skinhead later became associated with aggression and racism, the original skinheads were not politically motivated or violent.

Complicated cornrows

This is a traditional West African style where the hair is braided very close to the scalp. The style was brought to the United States by slaves and worn by both men and women. It regained popularity in the 1960s and the 1970s as part of the Black Power movement and is popular once again because of the spread of hip-hop culture.

Amazing Mohawk

This dramatic hairstyle—with the center of the hair long and spiked, and the sides often shaved—is usually associated with the Mohawk tribe of Native Americans. Punks adopted the Mohawk hairstyle in the 1970s, often dying their hair bright colors and shaping it into liberty spikes to resemble the Statue of Liberty in New York City.

No brush necessary

Dreadlocks are matted strands of hair, often associated with the Rastafarian religion that originated in Jamaica in the West Indies. They are usually formed by back combing the hair and not brushing it. The hair tangles as it grows and forms long, twisted strands that look like rope.

19

MAKE EARRINGS!

Want to add something fun and eye-catching to your outfit for a special occasion? All you need are a few items from a craft store!

You will need:

- 2 metal earring hooks
- 2 pieces of jewelry wire with looped ends
- round nose pliers
- assorted beads

1

Thread a bead onto the end of your jewelry wire.

2

Use your pliers to curl the straight end of the jewelry wire into a double knot.

3

Use your pliers to pull open the looped end of your earring hook.

4

Hook the loop of the jewelry wire onto the opened loop of the earring hook.

5

Use your pliers to squeeze the loop of the earring hook closed again. Congratulations, you have made your first earring! Repeat steps 1 to 5 to make the second earring.

Got it?

Experiment with different colors, numbers, and sizes of beads. If you find using the pliers difficult at first, ask an adult to help you with steps 2 and 3. Then try to complete steps 4 and 5 on your own. And keep at it. Making earrings gets easier with practice.

SKIN-TASTIC!

Many people love altering their appearance. Some do it permanently. Others prefer something temporary. Here are some of the most popular methods.

Ink for life

Tattooing is usually done with an electric tattoo machine. The machine pushes needles into the skin between 50 and 3,000 times a minute. The needles penetrate the skin by about 0.04 inches (1.0 millimeter), depositing a drop of insoluble ink with each puncture into the layer of skin called the dermis. The ink stays in place for a person's whole life. Tattoo artists should always use sterile, disposable needles to avoid infection.

Part-time tattoos

Harquus is a temporary paint that looks just like a tattoo. It is water resistant and does not penetrate or dye the skin. It lasts for a few days.

Put a ring in it

Piercing is when a hole is made in the skin so that a stud, a ring, or another type of jewelry can be worn. The hole is often made with a piercing gun. Ear piercing was started by tribes in South America and Africa as a way to protect against evil spirits thought to enter the body via the ears!

The hole truth

Stretching is the expansion of a healed piercing, usually in the ear. A taper (a rod that gets thicker at one end) is often used. In ancient times, stretched ears were a symbol of wealth. Rich merchants collected gold, which they melted down and turned into earrings. Gold is a heavy metal, so it stretched the ears. The longer their ears, the richer the merchants appeared!

harquus

ink tattoos

piercing

stretching

GOING GLOBAL

Amazing body decoration, from neck rings to face painting, exists around the world. Here are some of the most eye-catching examples.

South America

The Kayapo people live in the Amazon rain forest in South America. They mark their faces and bodies with tattoos that they believe guard against evil spirits thought to live in the forest. Some Kayapo men also insert disks into their lower lips to stretch the skin.

India

Indian weddings are very colorful events that last for several days. The bride wears outfits in colors, especially red, a color that is thought to bring good luck. She may also have henna patterns on her hands, forearms, legs, and feet. The bride often wears ornate earrings and forehead decorations.

New Zealand

Maori warriors used to scar and tattoo their faces with bone chisels to frighten their enemies. The less permanent

Tattooed Maori warriors *(left)* make faces to add to their fearsome appearance. Painting the body *(top)* is an art form in its own right.

tradition of face painting carries the same meanings of power and authority within a modern tribe.

Austria

In 1998 Austria hosted the first World Bodypainting Festival. The event has since grown to become the biggest festival of its kind with more than 200 artists and 30,000 visitors attending

Britain

The International London Tattoo Convention in London, England, has been running since 2005. It attracts more than 20,000 visitors from around the world, as well as famous tattoo artists, such as Robert Hernandez and Roberto Borsi.

United States

The Tattoo Art Museum in San Francisco, California, covers the history of U.S. tattooing. Run by well-known tattooist Lyle Tuttle, it houses antique tattoo guns, portraits of famous subjects, and sheets of historical tattoo artwork.

KAT VON D

THE STATS

Name: Katherine Von Drachenberg
Born: March 8, 1982
Place of birth: Monterrey, Mexico
Job: Tattoo artist, TV star

Among countless other tattoos, Kat has a sleeve design on both arms.

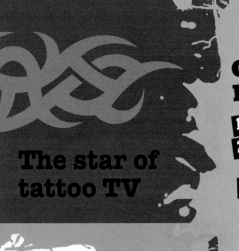

The star of tattoo TV

Career highlights

1996 did her first tattoo on a friend

2008 founded the Musink Tattoo Convention and Music Festival

2010 opened the Wonderland Gallery, an art gallery and boutique shop, next door to her tattoo parlor, High Voltage Tattoo

2010 Kat's second book, *The Tattoo Chronicles*, is published and reaches No. 3 on the *New York Times* best-seller list

Growing up

Kat was born in Mexico but moved to the United States with her family when she was just four years old. Growing up, Kat was always sketching pictures and designs. In her teens, she told her parents that she wanted to be a doctor like her father. But he was convinced that Kat had a natural skill for drawing. He encouraged her to pursue her talent and make a living out of art instead.

Tattoo culture

As a teenager, Kat was inspired by rock and punk music and by the fashion and lifestyle that went with them. She got her first tattoo while still in her teens and working in a tattoo parlor in San Bernardino, California. It was here that the customers christened her Kat Von D. Her love of music has led to Kat carrying tattoos of her favorite bands, including Guns N' Roses, AC/DC, and ZZ Top.

Getting a break on TV

Kat eventually found a job as a tattoo artist in a shop in Hollywood, California, where she met the tattoo artist Chris Garver. Chris left the shop to star in *Miami Ink*, a TV reality show about the everyday lives of tattoo artists and their customers. Six months later, he asked Kat to join him. She was the only woman on the show and a talented tattooist. Kat showed she had a talent for getting close to customers, understanding completely what they wanted, and how much their tattoos meant to them. She was such a hit with viewers that Kat was offered her own show in Los Angeles.

Superstar status

LA Ink, set in Kat's High Voltage Tattoo shop, has turned her into a celebrity. The show has been running since 2007 and is a big hit, watched by more than three million people. Kat has tattooed famous people including *Lost* actor Dominic Monaghan and Steve-O and Bam Margera from the hit MTV show *Jackass*. She recently launched a range of makeup for the beauty store Sephora. Her 2009 book *High Voltage Tattoo*, a collection of her artwork and tattoos, reached No. 6 on the *New York Times* best-seller list. Maybe sometimes parents really do know best!

Actress Ling Bai added tattoo cool to her style when she wore an Ed Hardy jacket to a *Star* magazine party.

TATTOOS MEAN BUSINESS

In the last 50 years, tattooing has gone from the underground to the mainstream. Designs by tattooists such as Ed Hardy and Sailor Jerry are being used to sell playing cards, clothes, and shoes! Tattooing is big business.

Starting the trend

Ed Hardy is one of the world's highest-profile tattooists. Born in California in 1945, Ed was a gifted artist and studied for a degree in printmaking before deciding to follow his first love: tattooing.

Ed's mix of traditional Asian and American characters quickly made him a familiar name in the tattoo community. Thanks to a business partnership with French marketing expert Christian Audigier, Ed's colorful designs have fans around the world.

Ed's artwork has been used on everything from T-shirts and baseball caps to sneakers. Not only is his business worth $20 million a year, but collectors are also lining up to buy his original prints for their walls.

Fellow tattoo artist

Ed's teacher was a tattooist named Sailor Jerry. Born Norman Keith Collins in Nevada in 1911, he joined the U.S. Navy at the age of 19 and traveled the world. Sailor Jerry's tattoo skills were heavily influenced by the same areas of the South Pacific that Captain Cook had visited. His groundbreaking designs proved very popular in the United States and are also being used to sell products. Converse, which makes casual shoes and sneakers, used Jerry's images for a range of high-top shoes. Jerry died in 1973, but his artwork has been collected in books that sell for between $300 and $400.

Worldwide profits

By successfully using the rebellious imagery of tattoo artists to sell products, companies have made tattooing more noticeable. More than 40 million Americans have a tattoo. Many of the ones who don't, probably own an Ed Hardy T-shirt!

AMAZING BODIES!

Check out the surprising—and sometimes painful—ways some people have ended up in the record books.

LONGEST SESSION

Who: Stephen Grady and Melanie Grieveson
When: 2006
Where: Wodonga, Australia
What: Longest tattoo session
How: Grady and Grieveson each spent 43 hours and 50 minutes in the tattooist's chair to break the world record!

MOST TATTOOED MAN

Who: Lucky Diamond Rich
When: Since 2006
Where: Sydney, Australia
What: World's most tattooed person
How: Street entertainer Lucky has spent thousands of hours in the tattooist's chair. His entire body is covered in black ink, including his eyelids and even his gums! He has now started having white designs tattooed on top of the black.

HAIR RAISING!

Who: Eric Hahn
When: 2008
Where: Omaha, Nebraska
What: World's tallest Mohawk
How: Eric's Mohawk was a massive 27 inches (69 centimeters), beating the old world record by more than 3 inches (8 cm)!

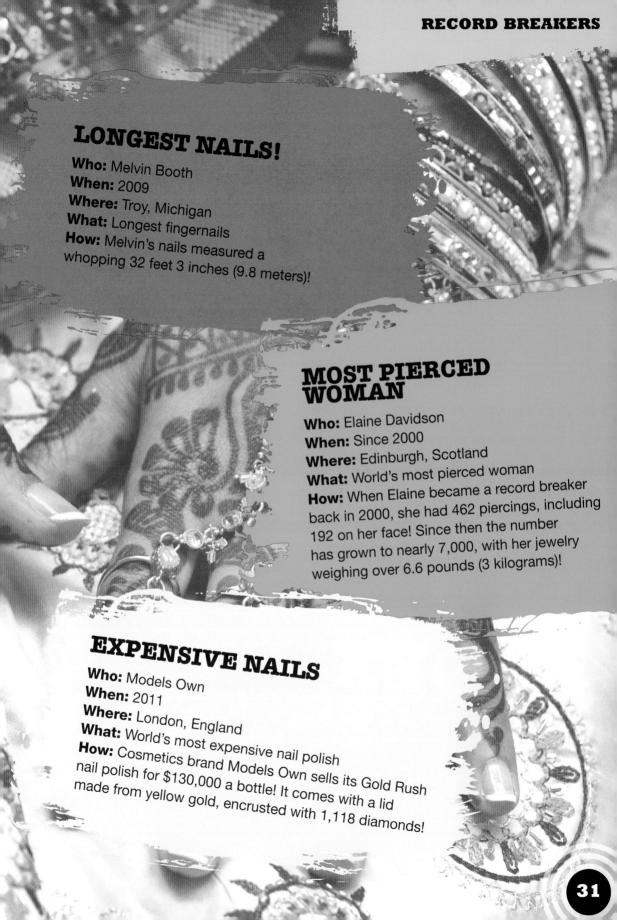

LONGEST NAILS!

Who: Melvin Booth
When: 2009
Where: Troy, Michigan
What: Longest fingernails
How: Melvin's nails measured a whopping 32 feet 3 inches (9.8 meters)!

MOST PIERCED WOMAN

Who: Elaine Davidson
When: Since 2000
Where: Edinburgh, Scotland
What: World's most pierced woman
How: When Elaine became a record breaker back in 2000, she had 462 piercings, including 192 on her face! Since then the number has grown to nearly 7,000, with her jewelry weighing over 6.6 pounds (3 kilograms)!

EXPENSIVE NAILS

Who: Models Own
When: 2011
Where: London, England
What: World's most expensive nail polish
How: Cosmetics brand Models Own sells its Gold Rush nail polish for $130,000 a bottle! It comes with a lid made from yellow gold, encrusted with 1,118 diamonds!

GET MORE INFO

Books

Barnes, Jennifer Lynn. *Tattoo*. New York: Random House, 2008. This novel tells the story of four teens who get temporary tattoos—as well as supernatural powers to fend off an evil enemy.

Gay, Kathlyn. *Body Marks: Tattooing, Piercing, and Scarification*. Minneapolis: Twenty-First Century Books, 2002. This book provides a broad history of body decoration through time.

Glicksman, Jane. *Fun Fingers, Fancy Feet*. Los Angeles: Lowell House, 2000. This book offers info about nail care and nail designs.

Nagle, Jeanne. *Tattoo Artists*. New York: Rosen Publishing Company, 2008. This book describes the work of various artists in the tattoo industry.

Websites

Body Piercing
http://kidshealth.org/teen/your_body/ body_art/body_piercing_safe.html
Information about body piercing is available through this site.

Nail Designs
http://www.nailpro.com/step-by-step
This website has step-by-step instructions to make some amazing nail designs.

To Tattoo or Not?
http://kidshealth.org/teen/your_body/ skin_stuff/safe_tattooing.html
This website gives kids who are thinking about getting a permanent tattoo information about the process and the risks. (In many states, parental permission is required if a person is under 18.)

INDEX